Mermaid and Unicorn Dolphin Coloring Book

Cute Mermaid and unicorn dolphin Coloring Page for girls and Kids

- ❖ This fun and inspirational Mermaid and Unicorn Dauphin Coloring Book is designed to everyone.

- ❖ With 60 pages, this Mermaid and Unicorn Dauphin Coloring Book will help build confidence while inspiring and entertaining.

- ❖ Mermaid and unicorn dauphin coloring book is a fun and creative way to nurture creativity and confidence. Perfect for girls women boy men who like to write, color, doodle and express themselves creatively.

- ❖ The pages in Mermaid and Unicorn Dauphin Coloring Book are single-sided to prevent bleed-through, and so that pages can be removed and displayed without losing an image on the back.
- ❖
    - In Mermaid and Unicorn Dauphin Coloring Book we have carefully designed each page to be entertaining and suitable for every children and girl.

Mermaids
and
Unicorns
Coloring
Book

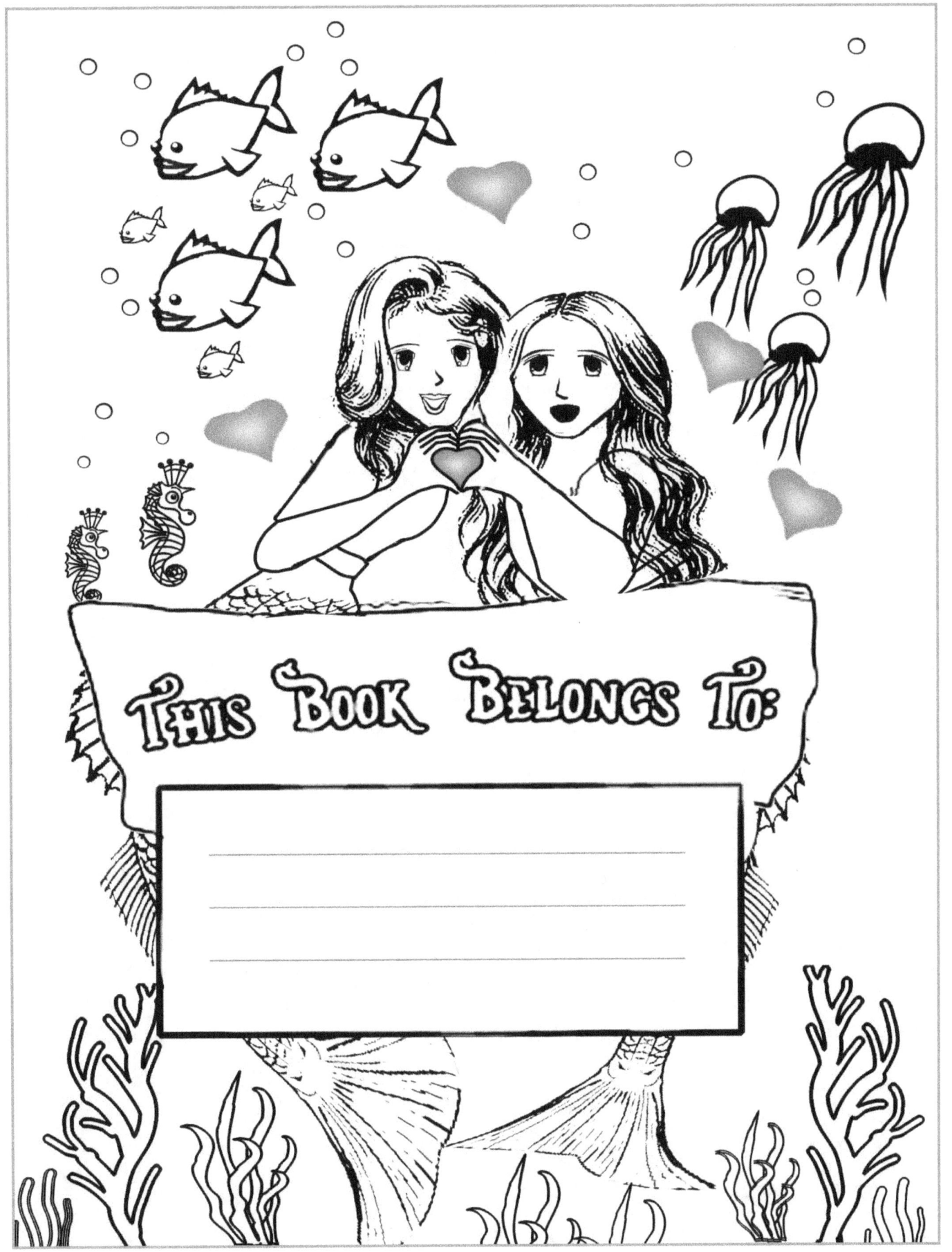

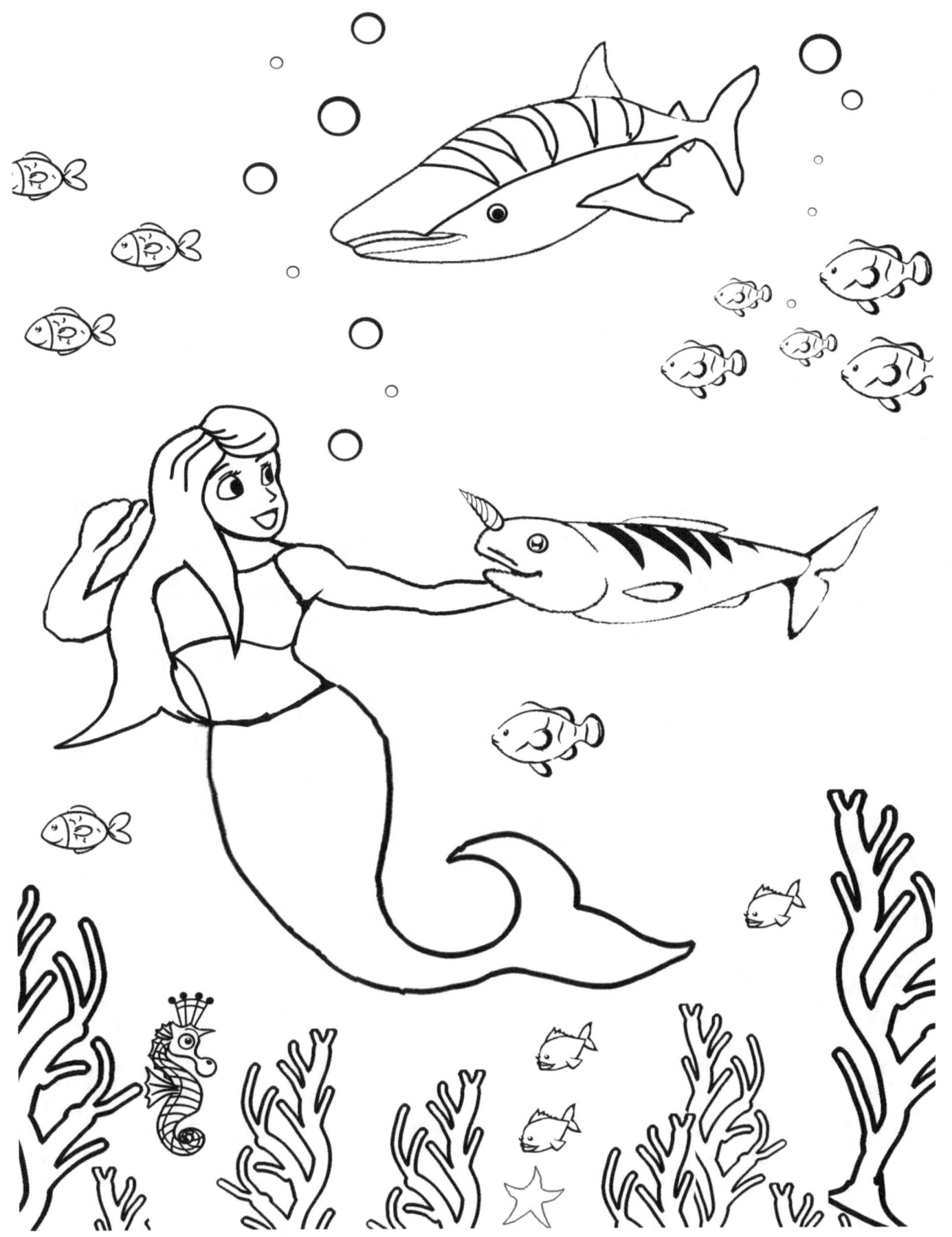

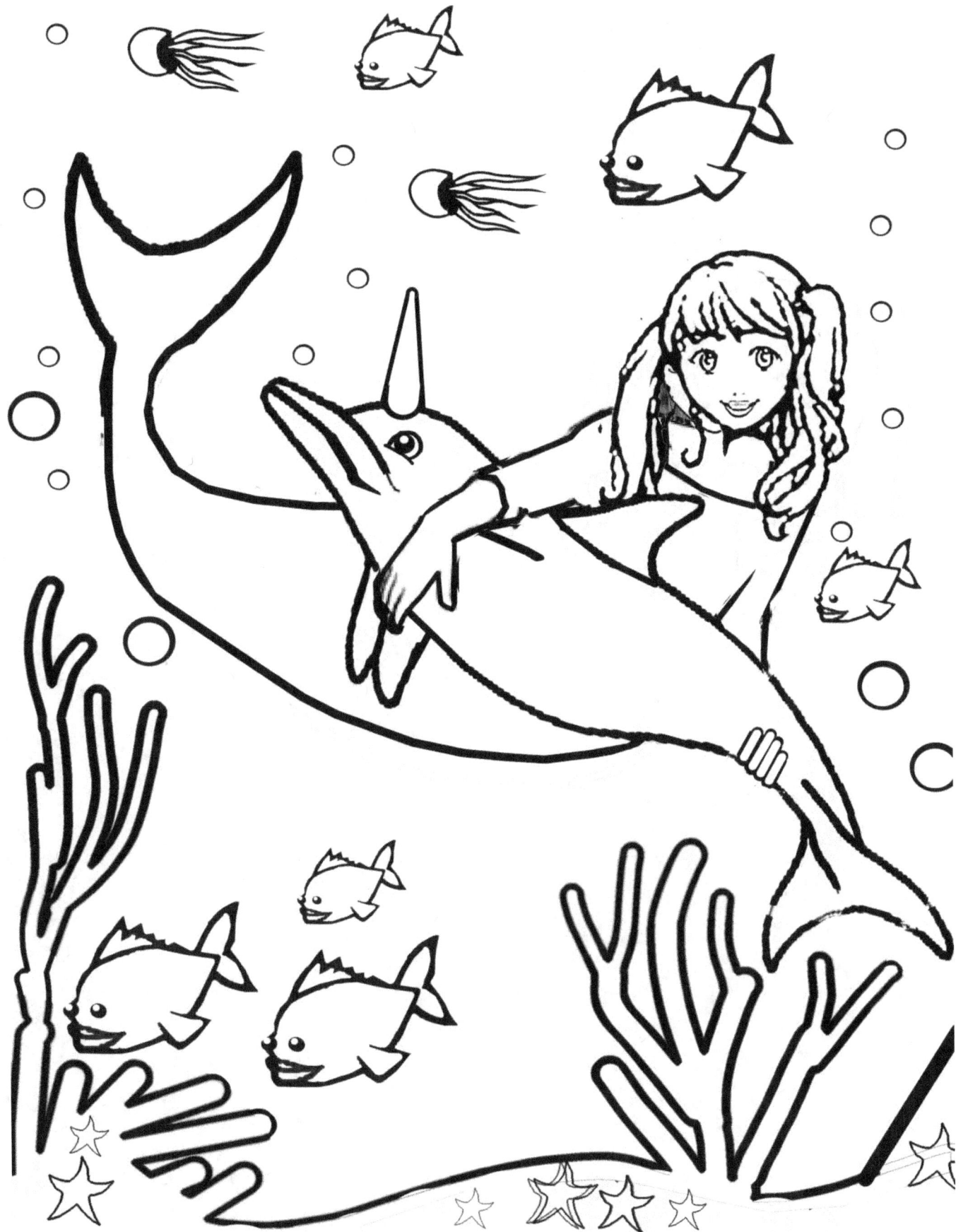

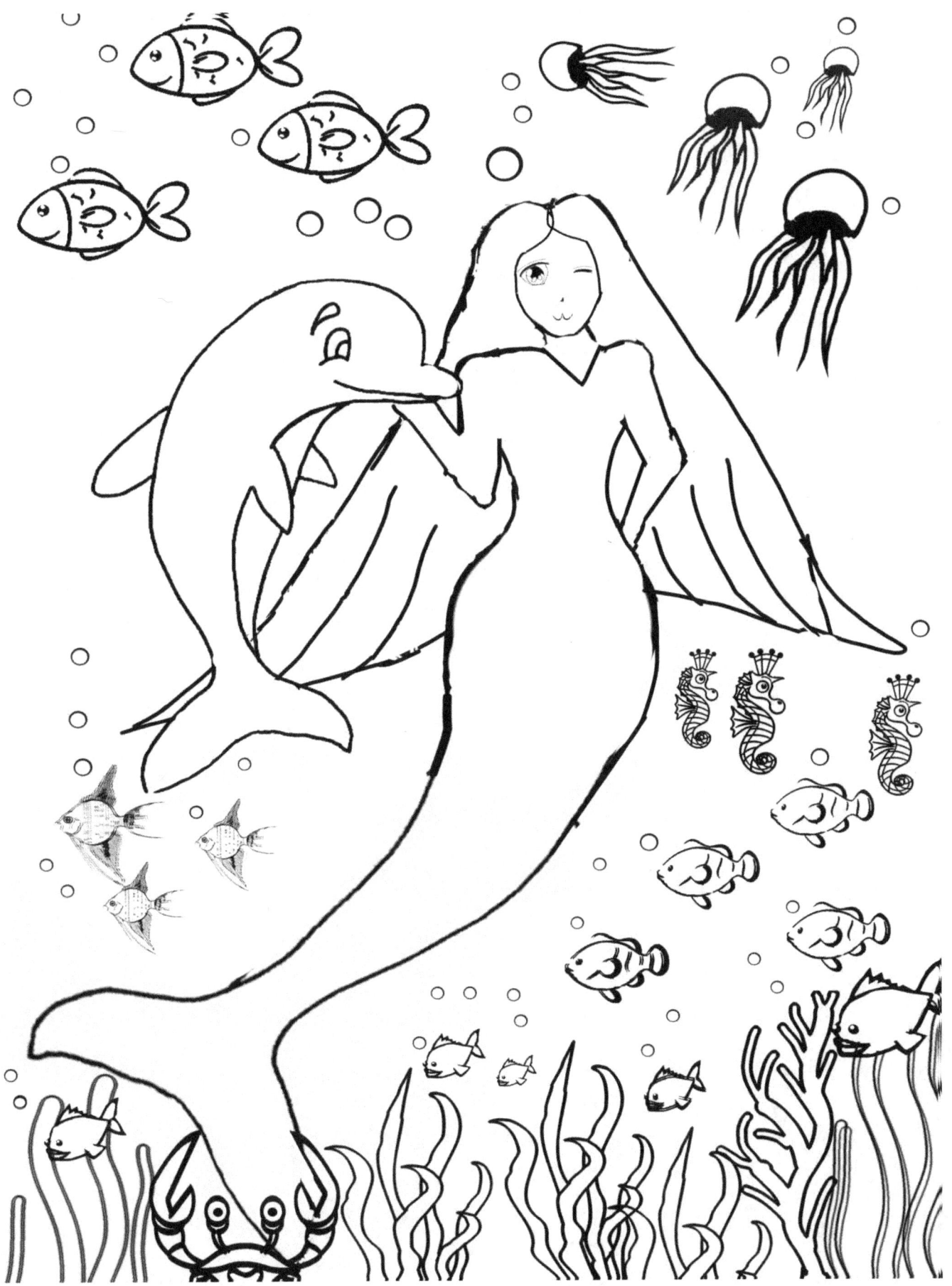

Memoirs of a Sailors Daughter

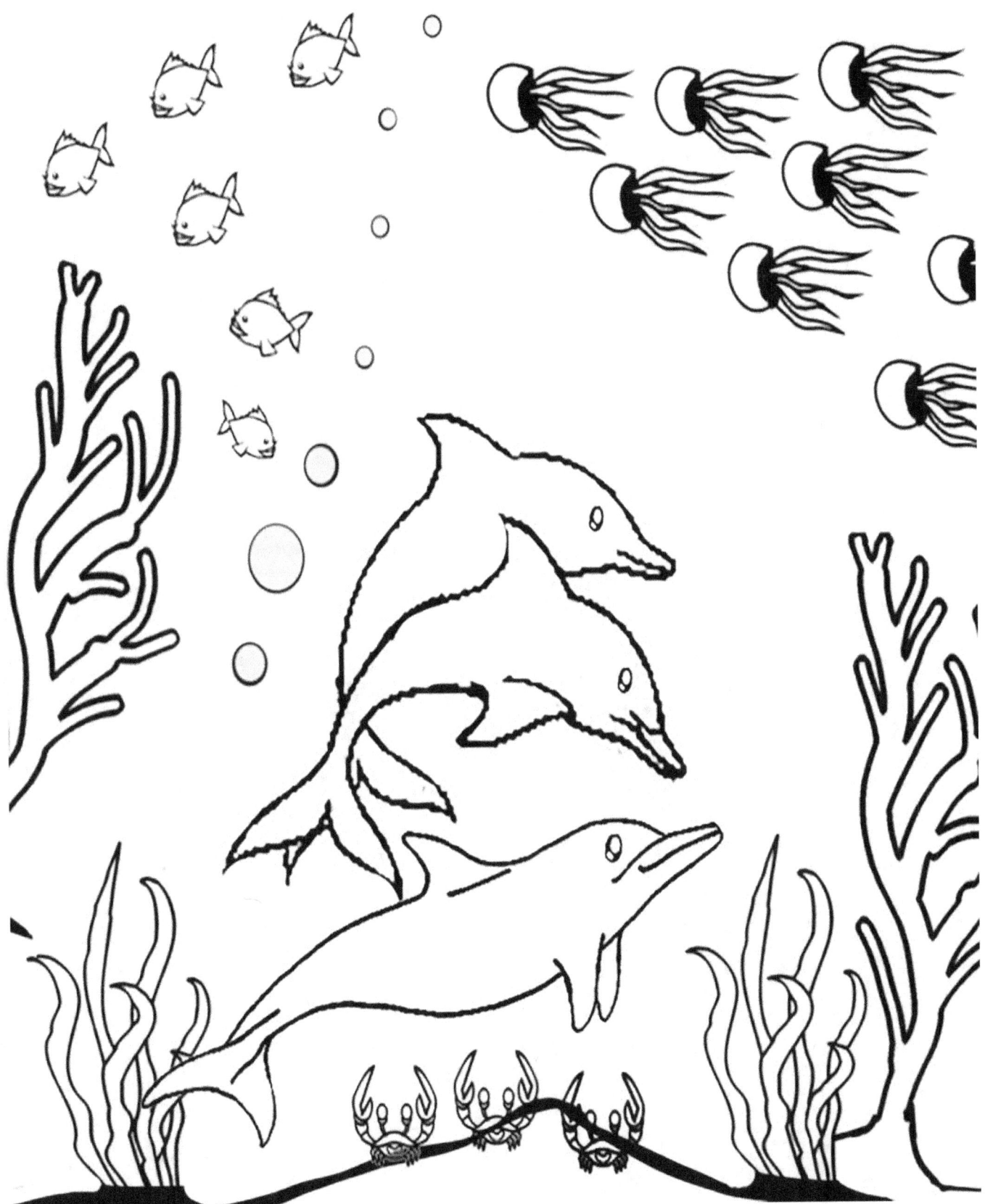

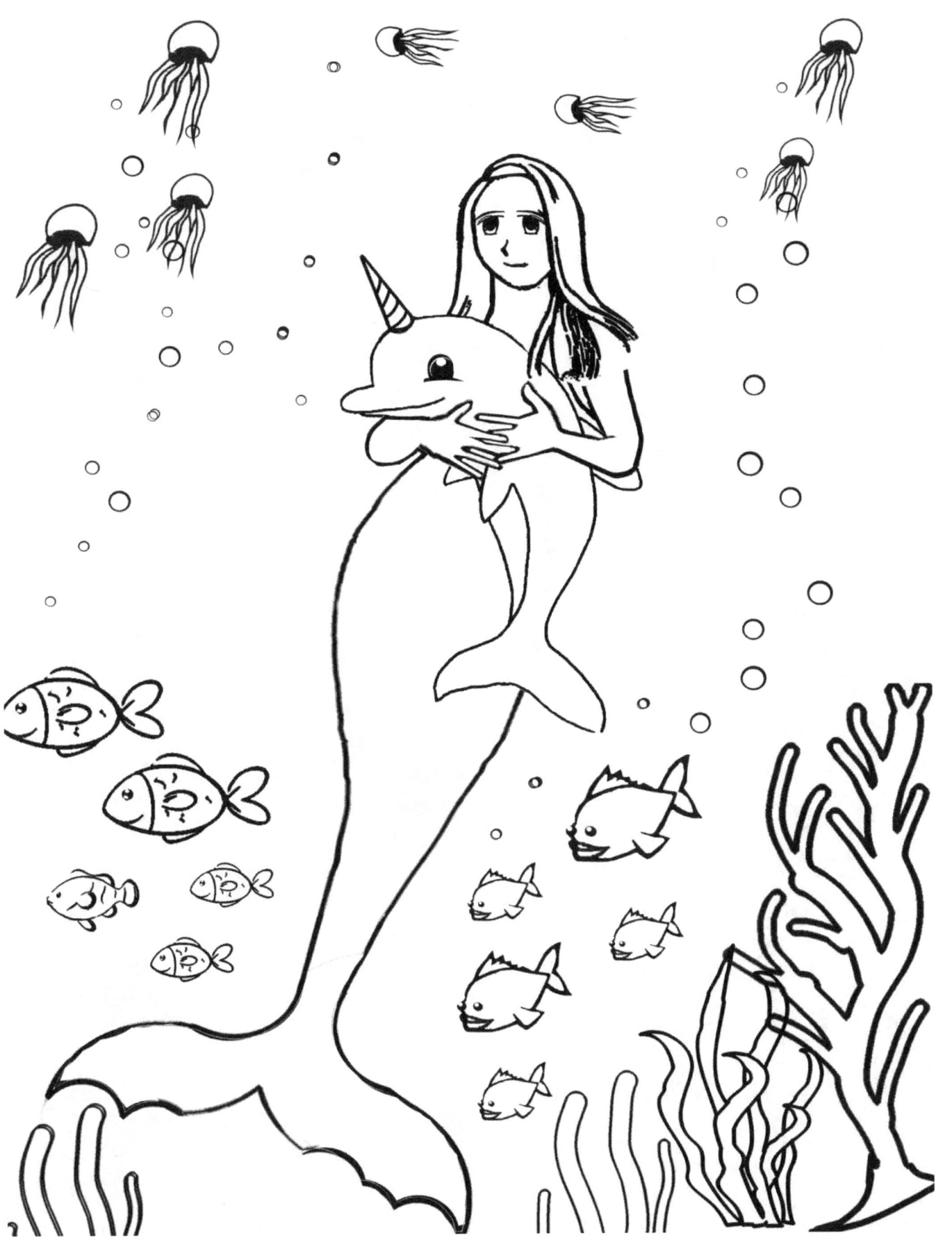

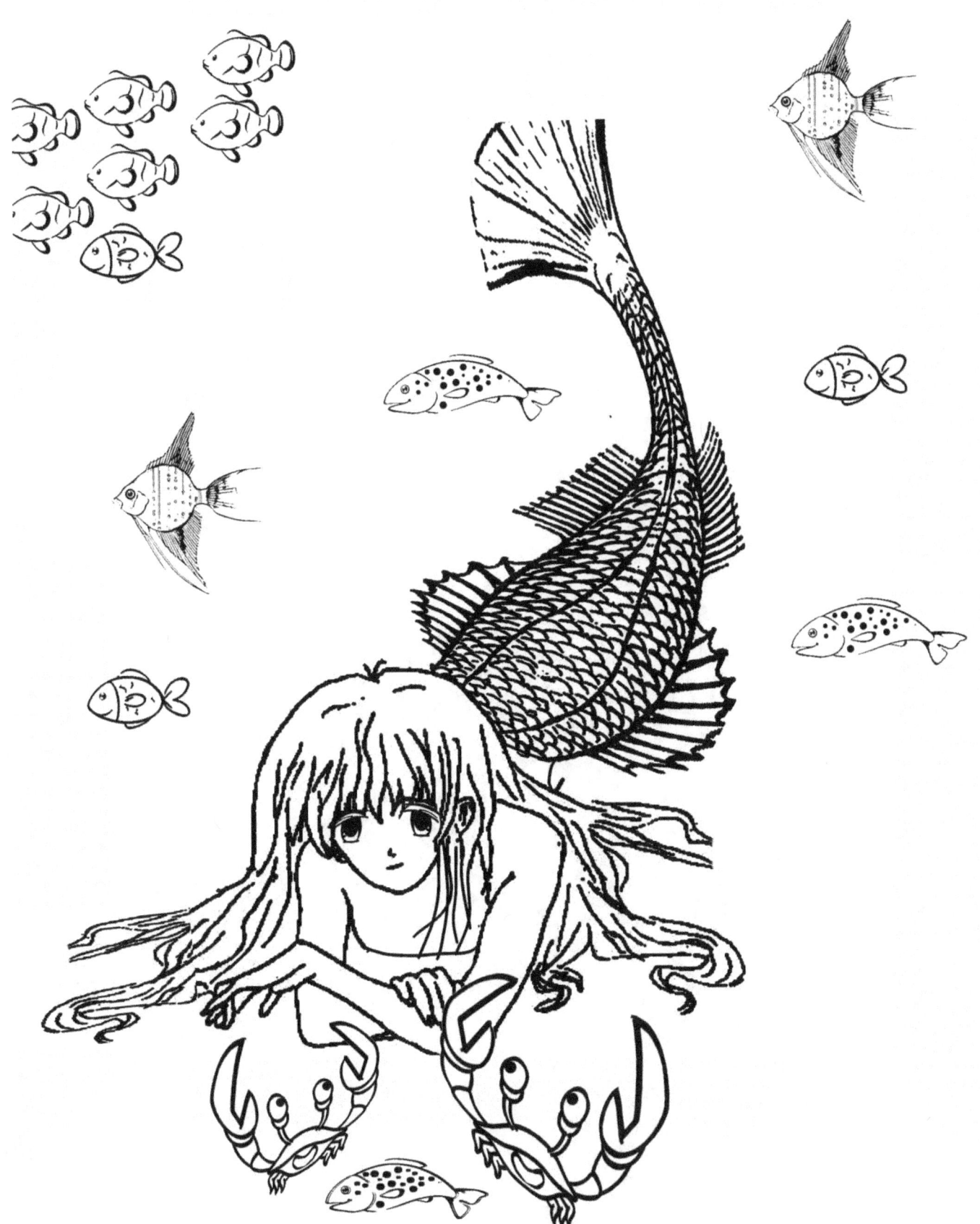

Mermaid
and
Unicorn
dabble
company
Book

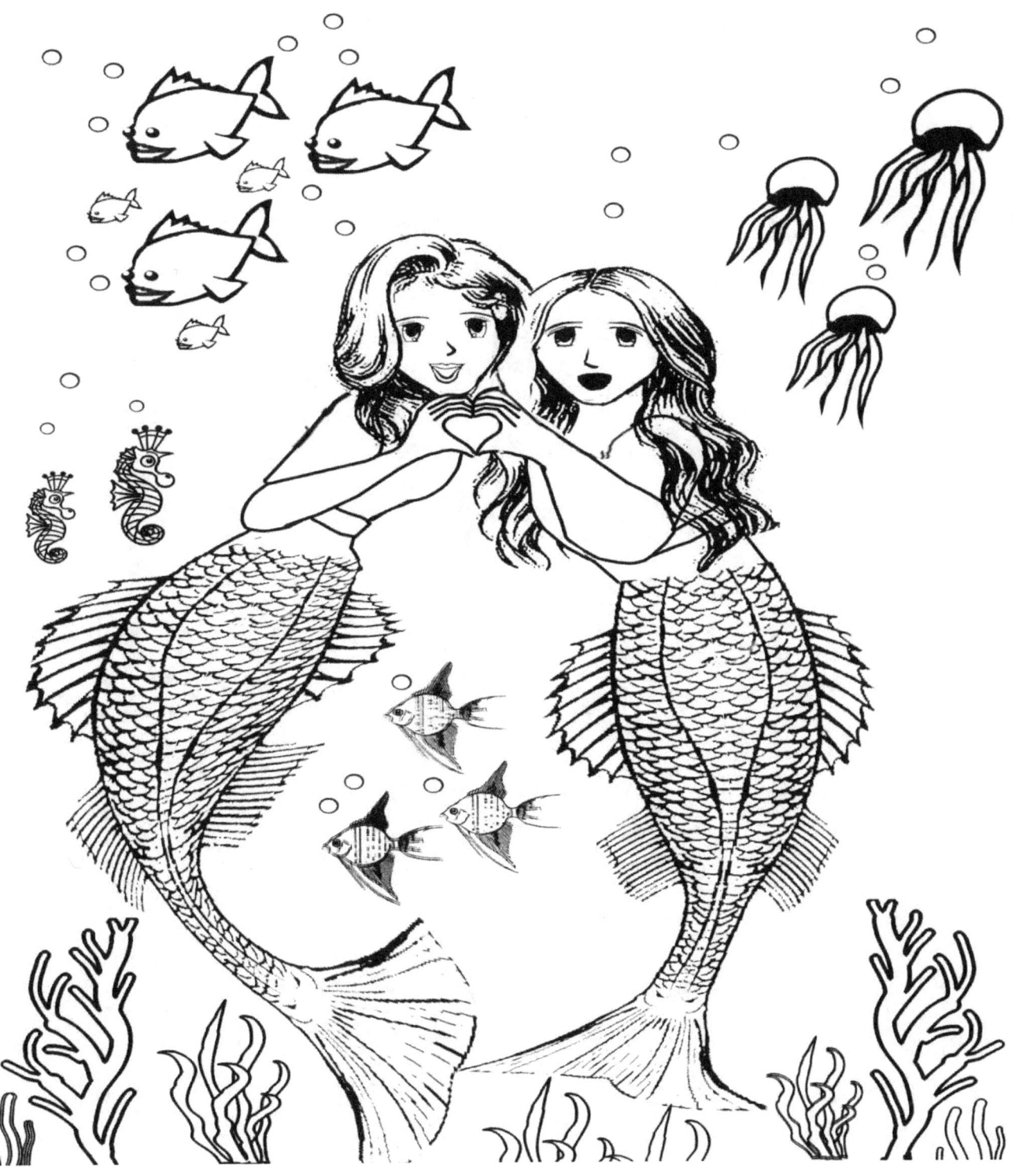

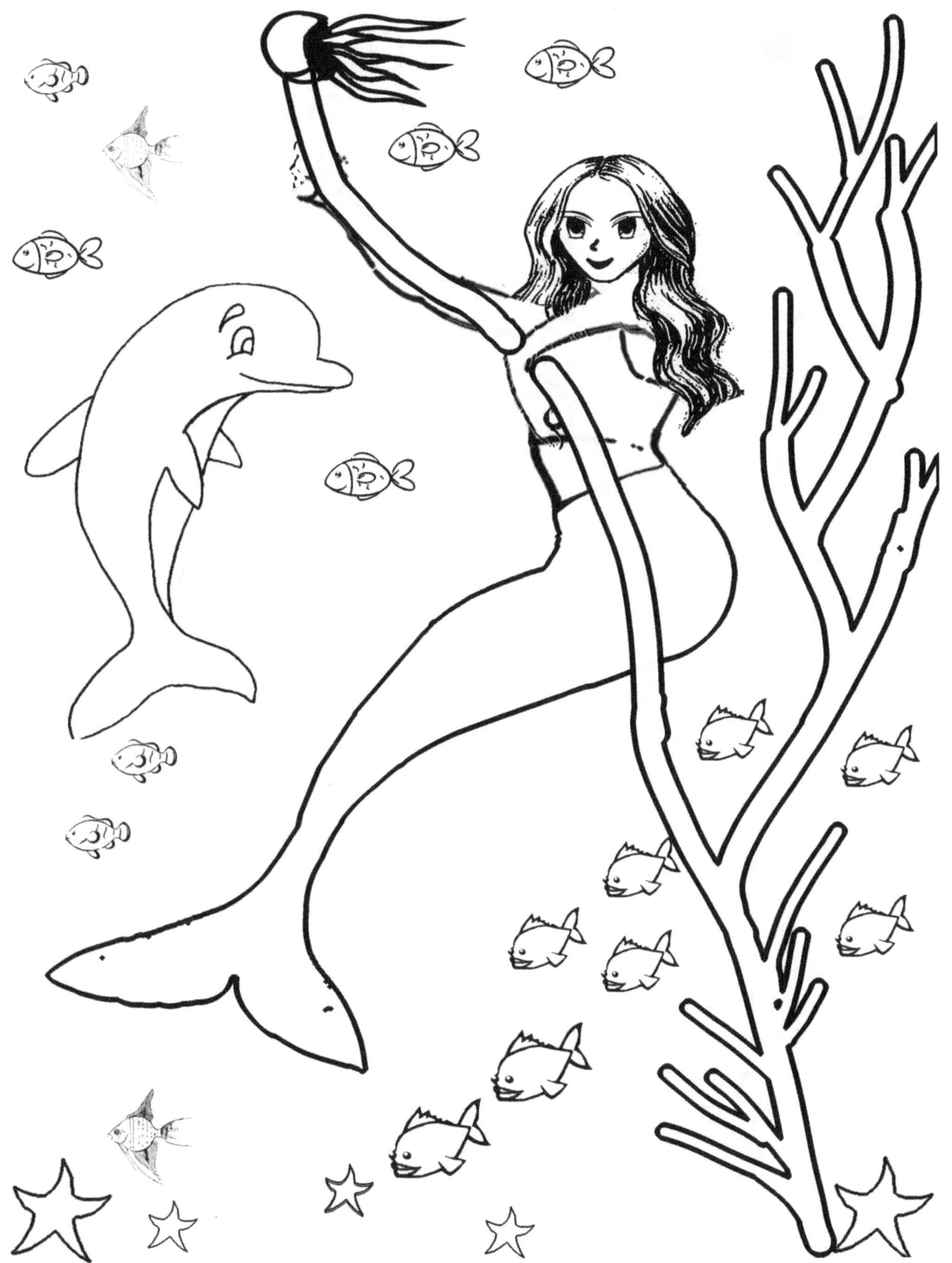

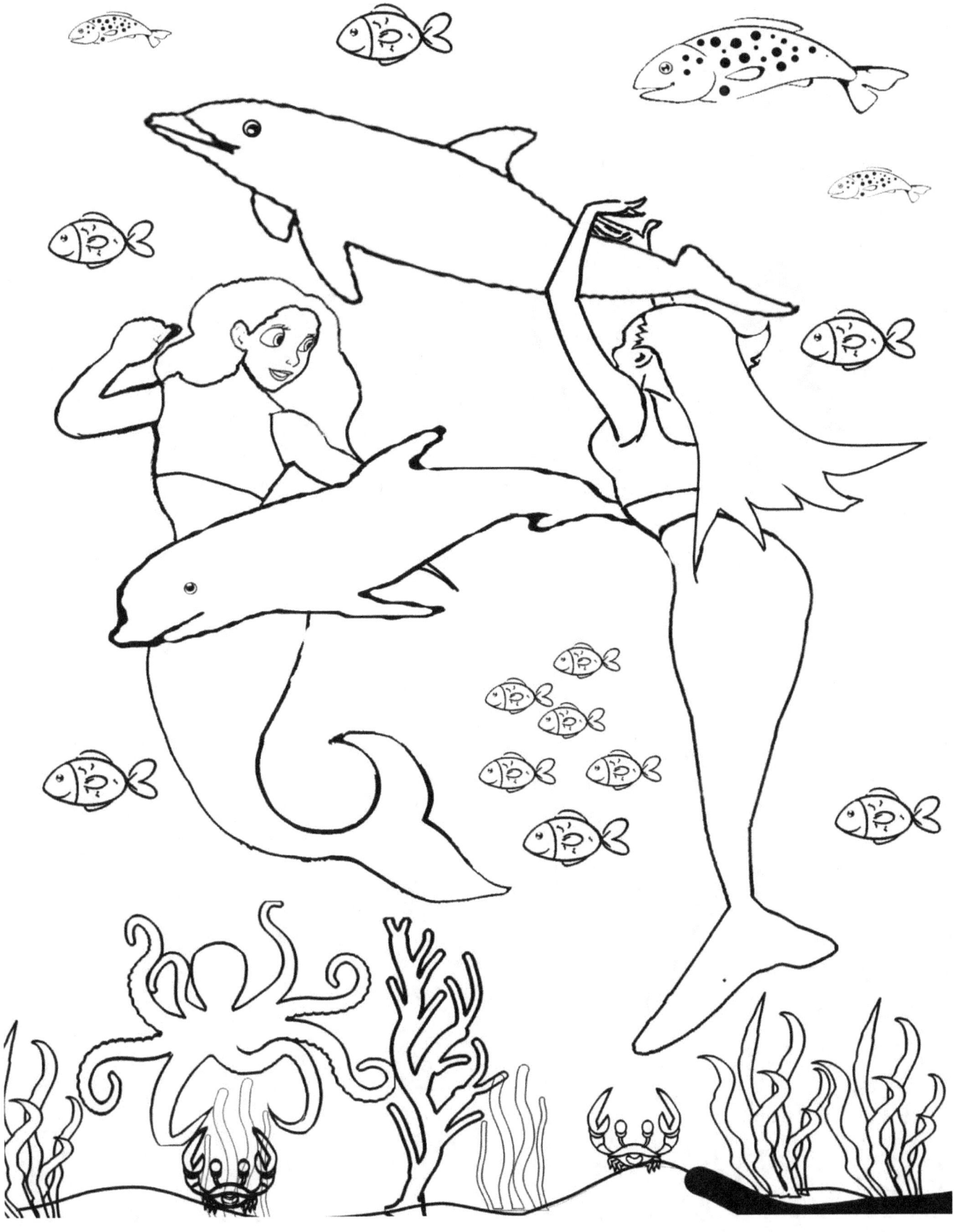

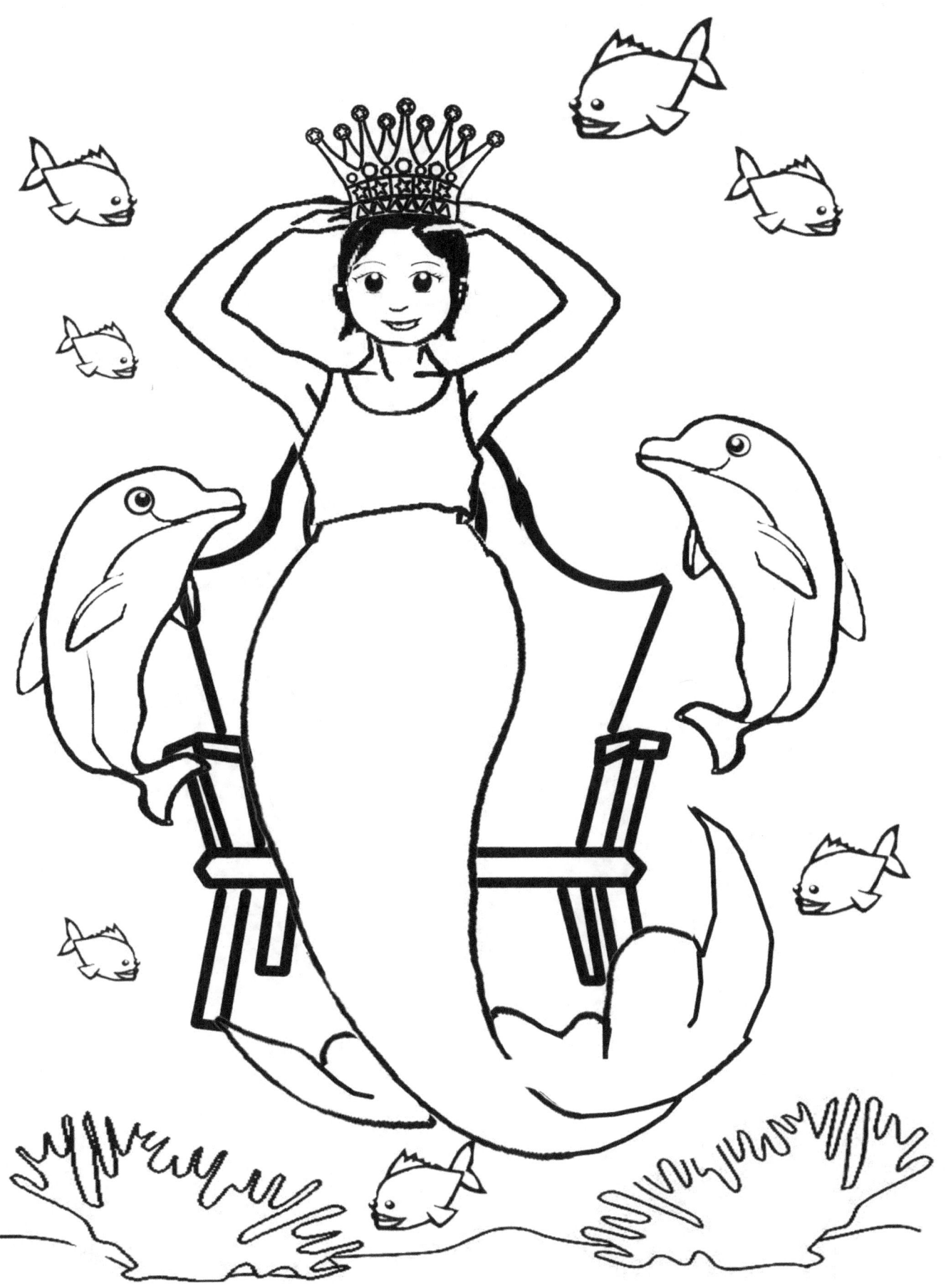

Mermaid
and
Unicorn
Dolphin
Coloring
Book

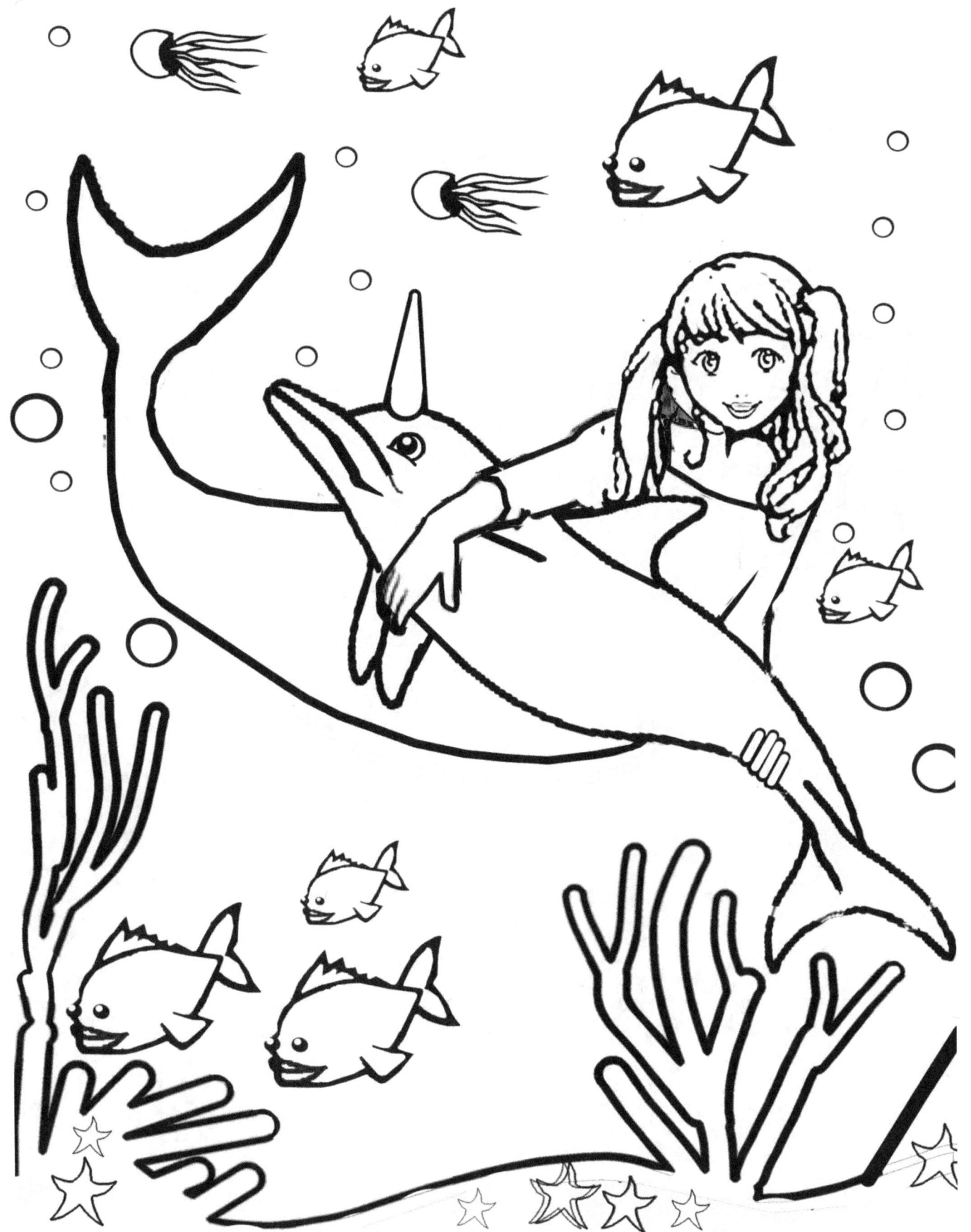

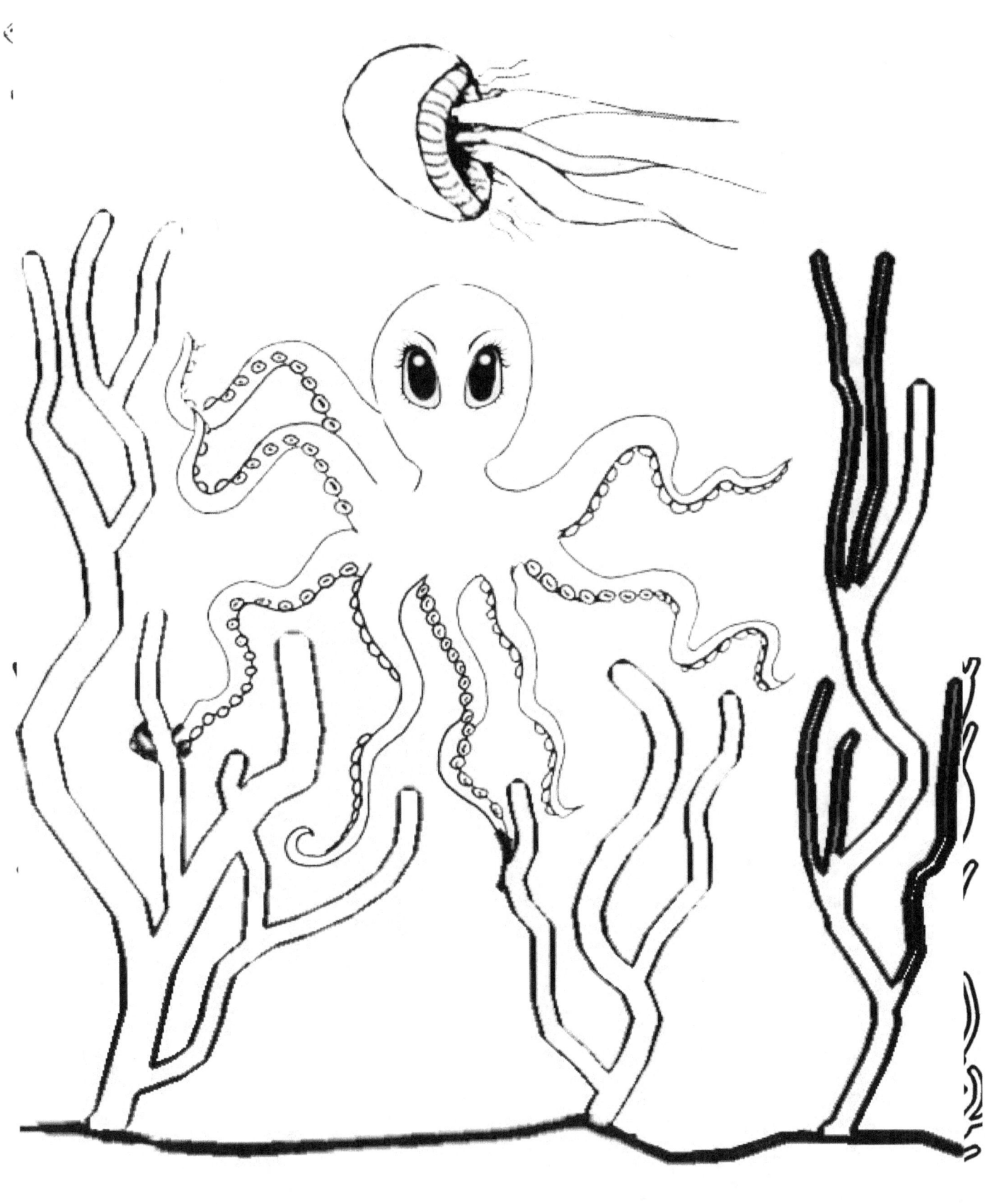

Mermaid
and
Unicorn
Dolphin
Coloring
Book

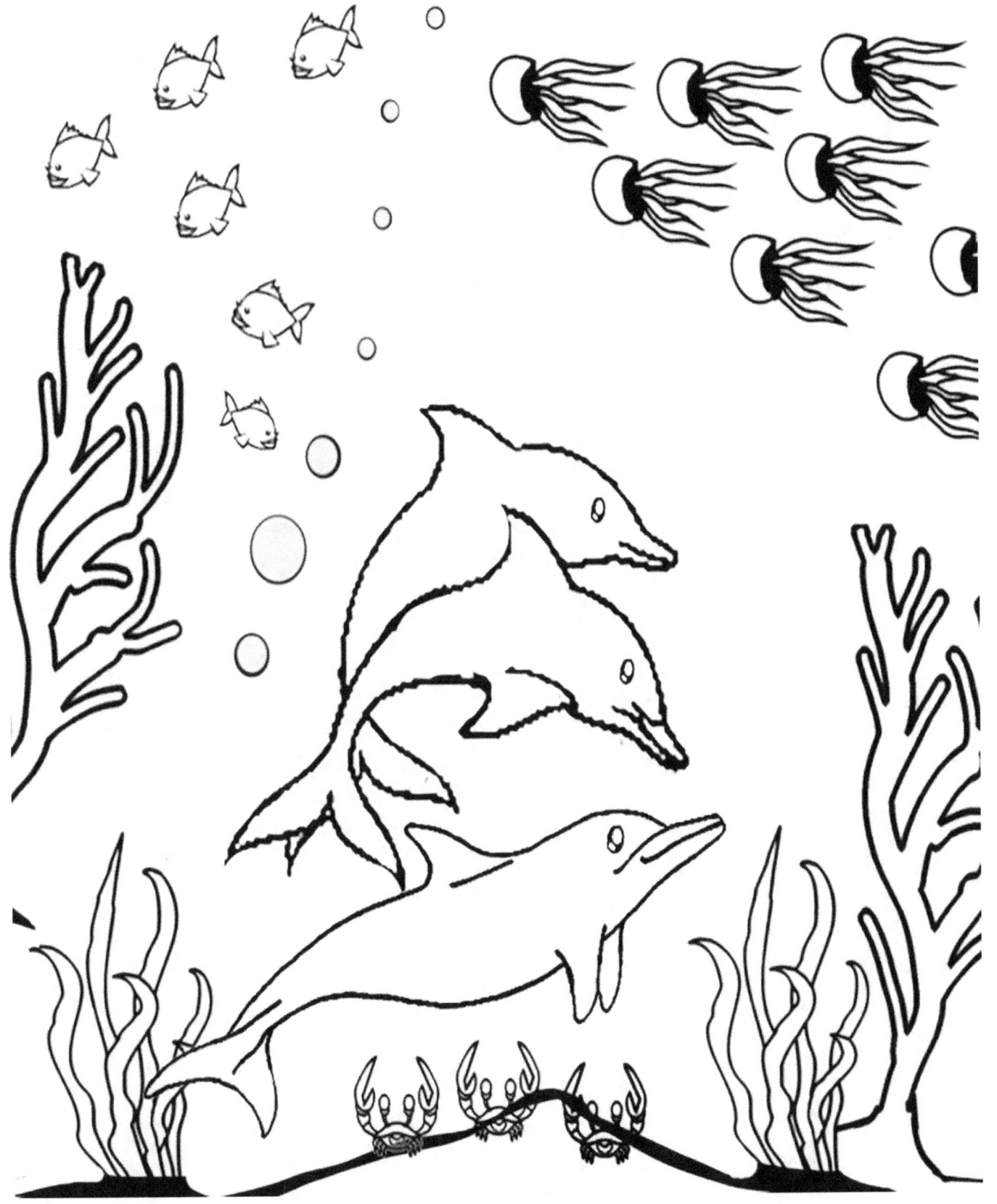

Mermaid and Dolphin Coloring Book

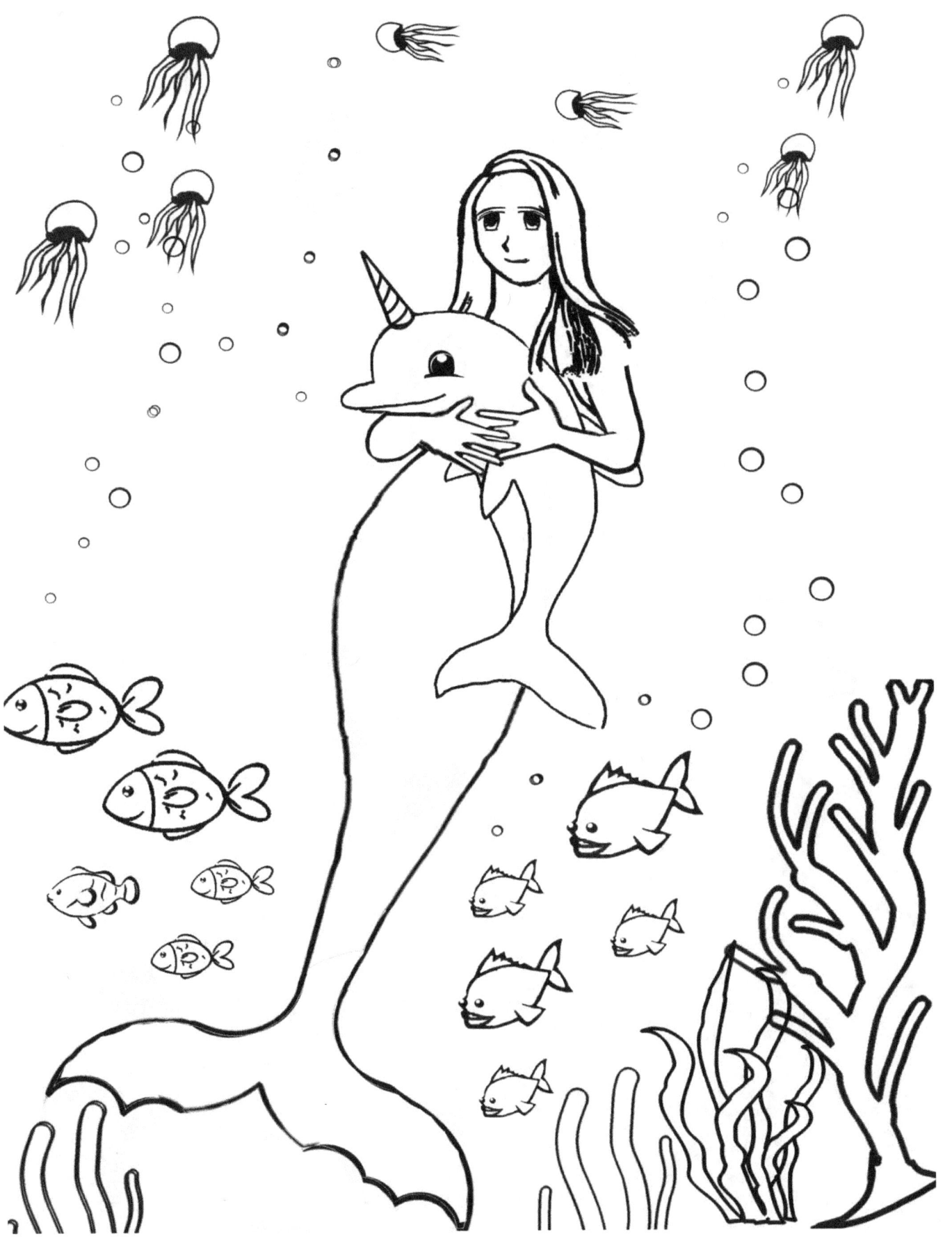

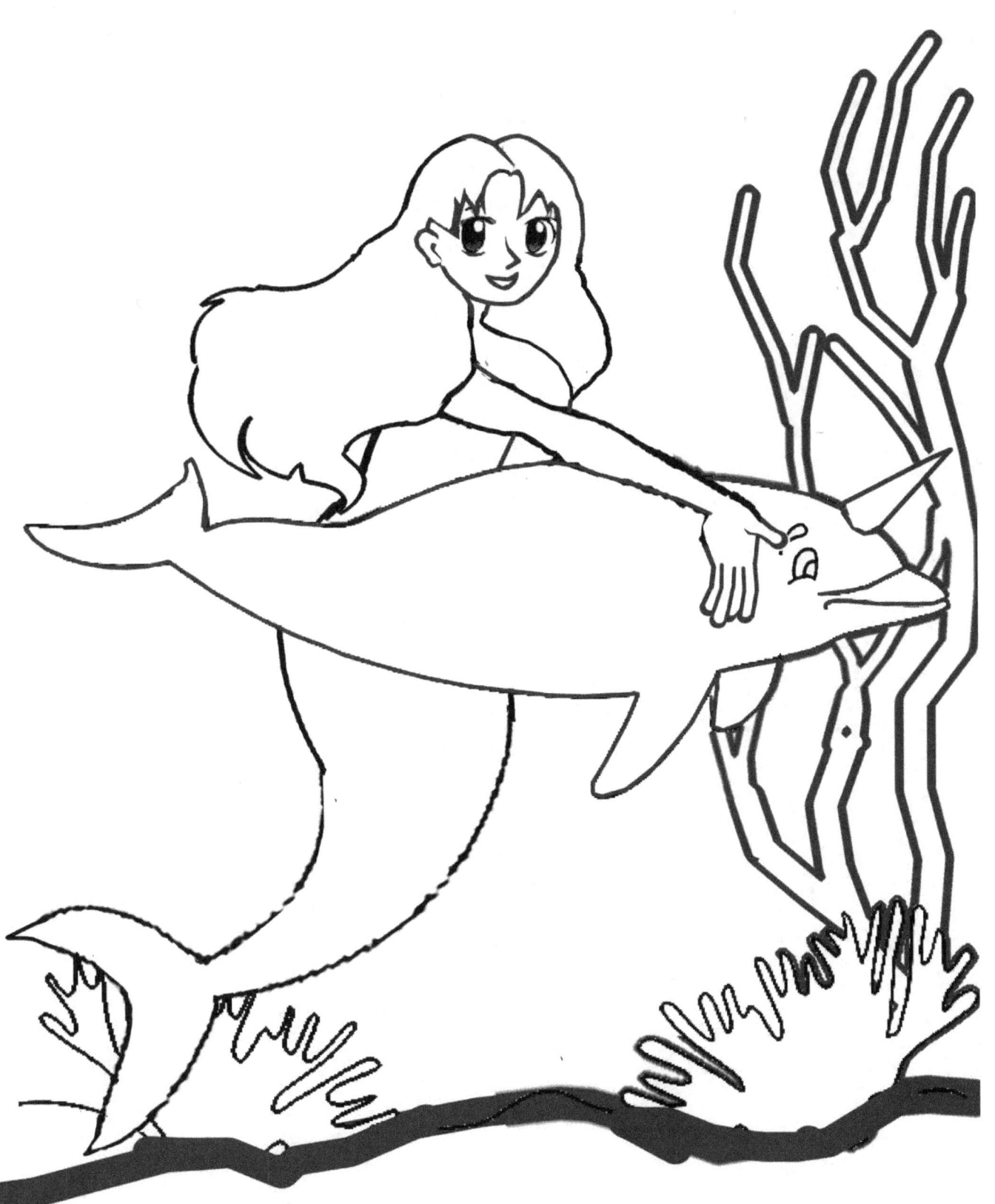

Inventors and Inventions

Teaching Resource Book

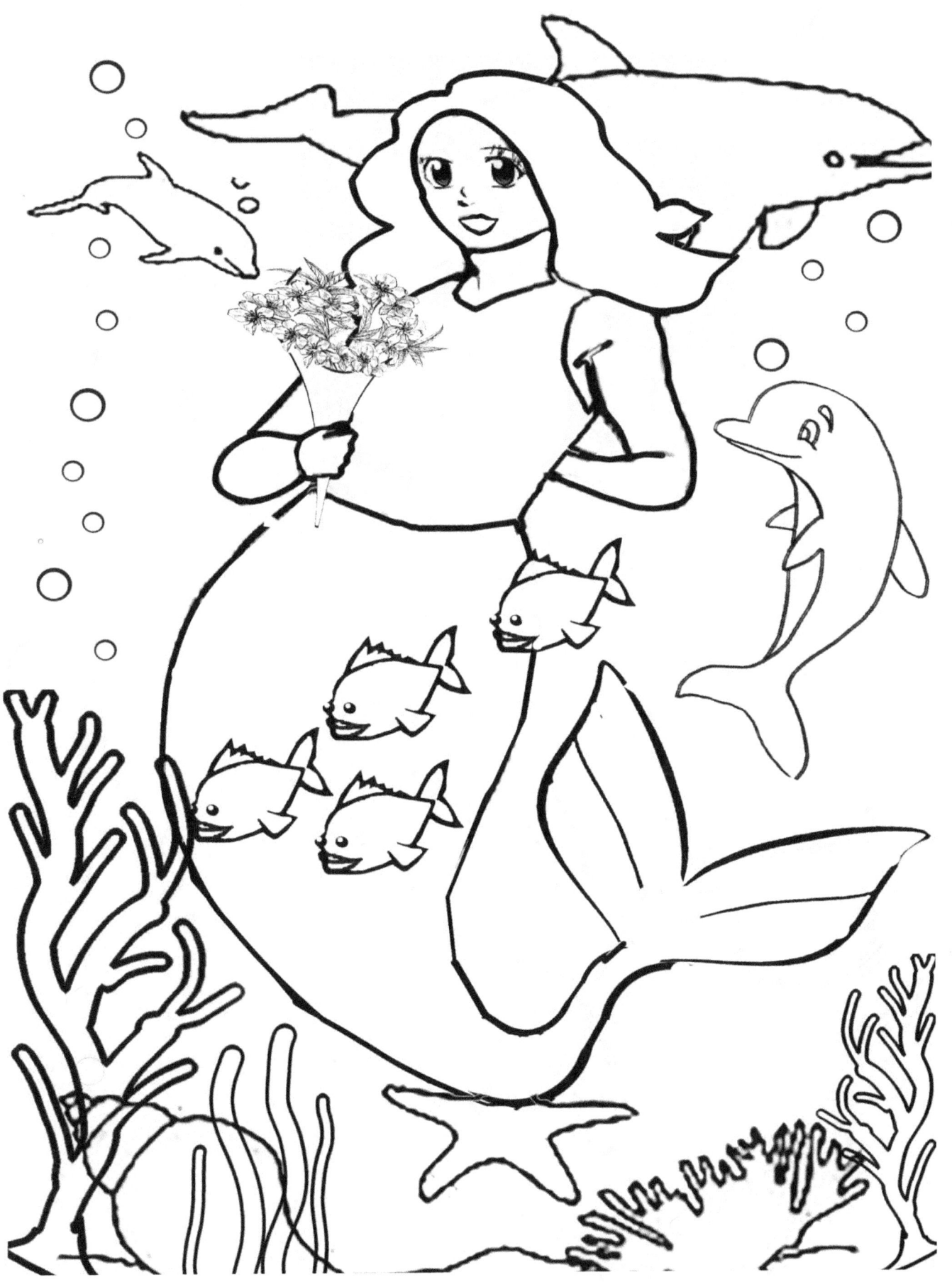

Mercato
and
Shoppes
Stenciling
Designs

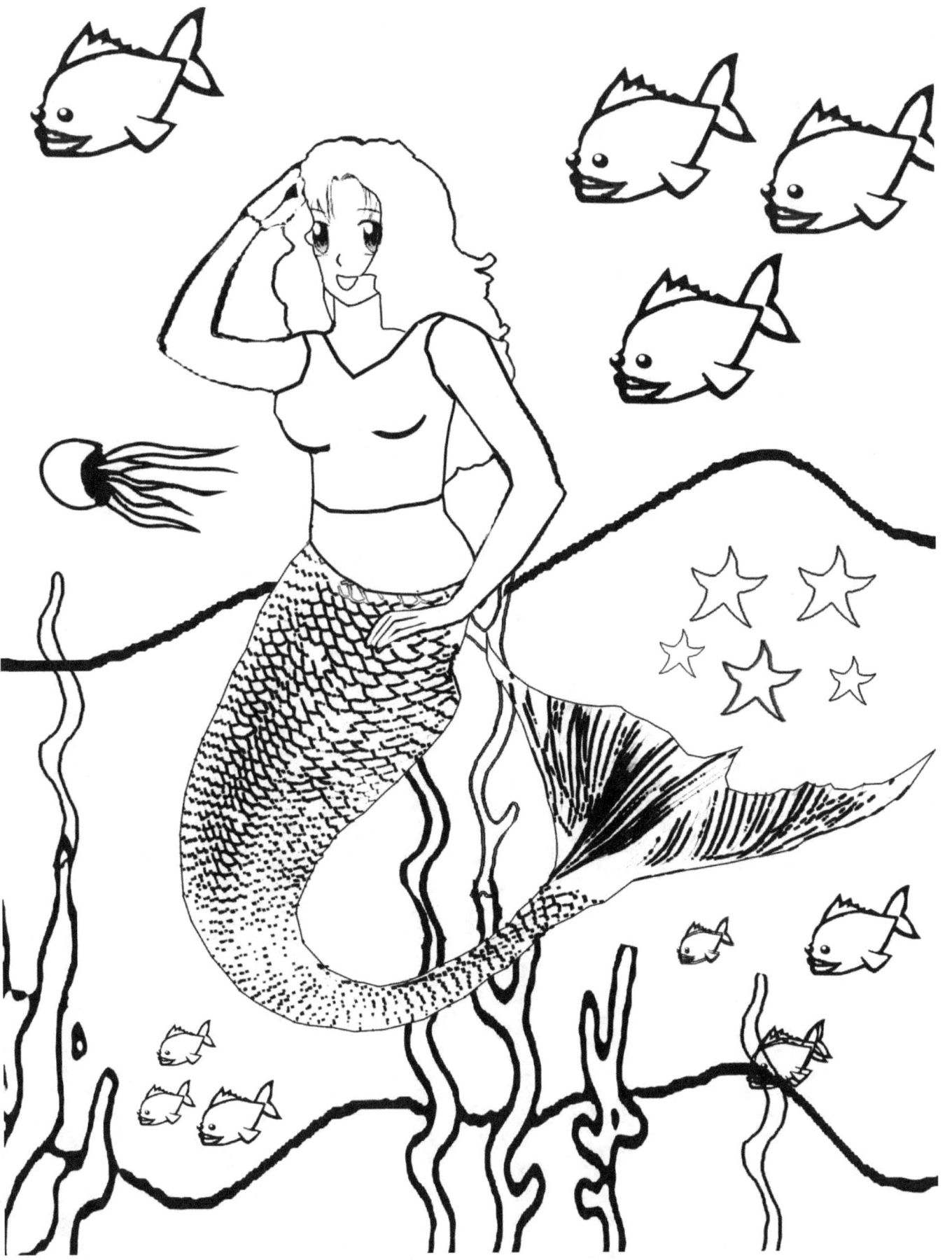

Mermaid
and
Unicorn
Dolphin
Coloring
Book

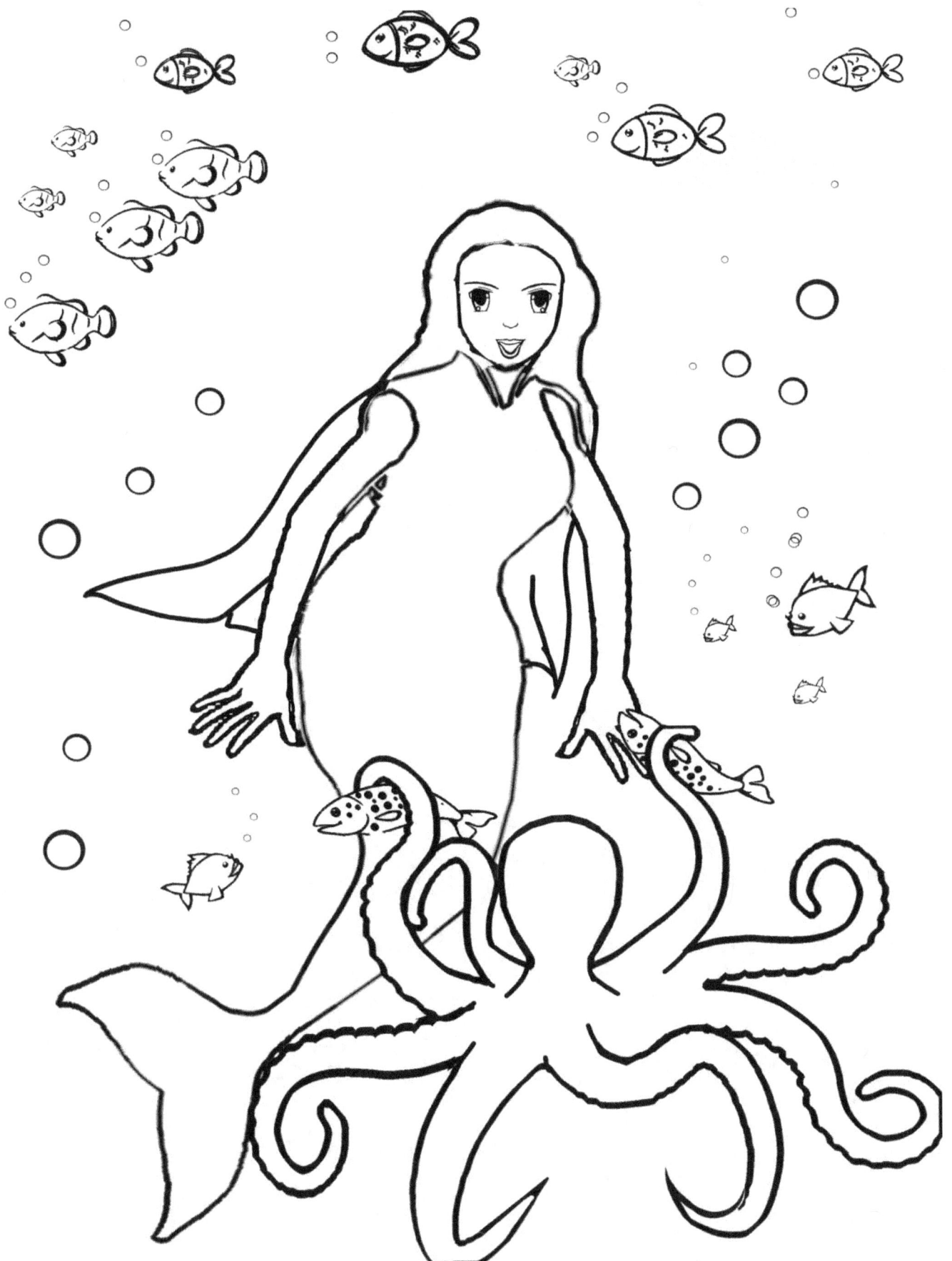

Methods
and
Literature
Selection
Protocols
Book

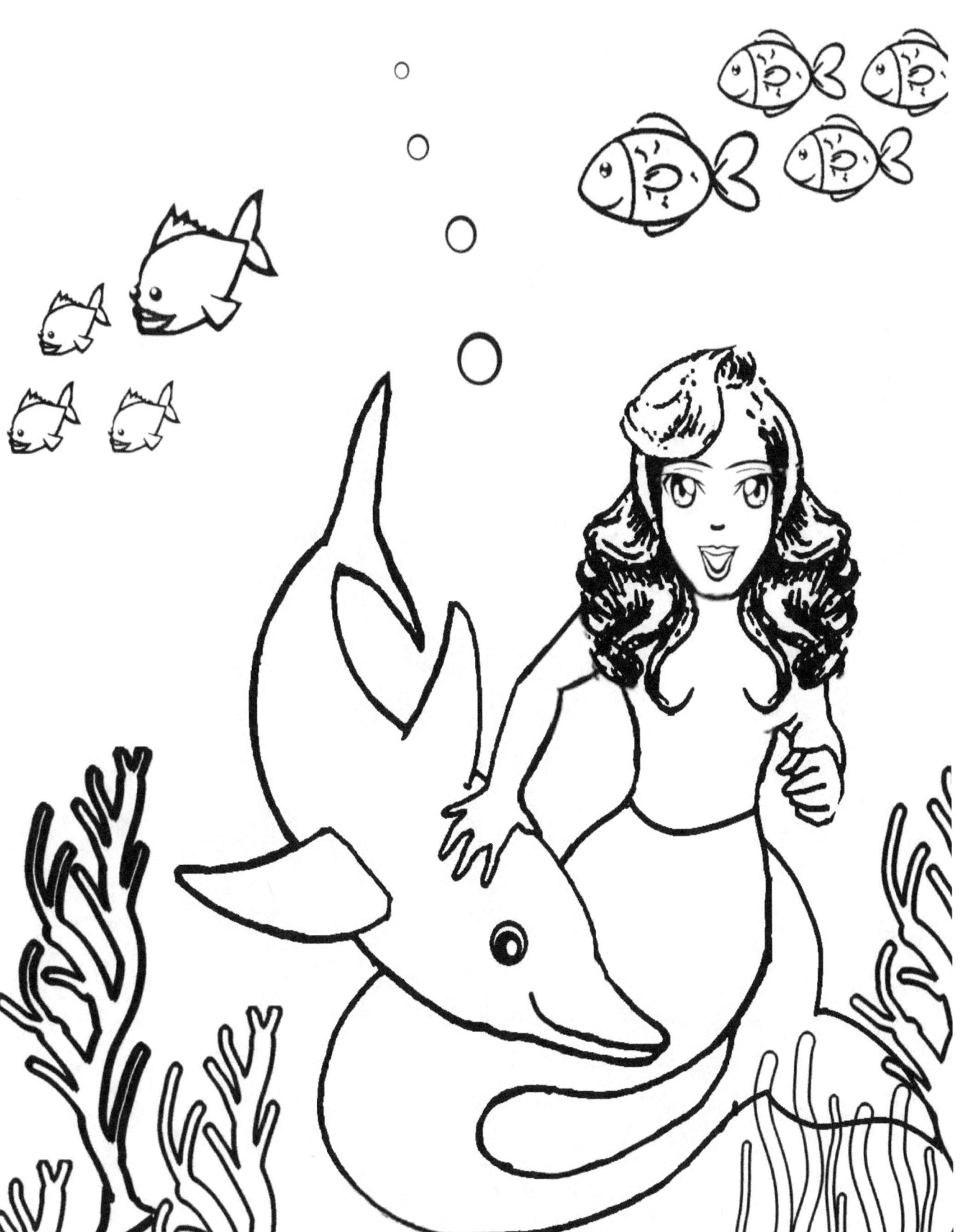

Mermaid
and
Unicorn
Stories
Volume
Two

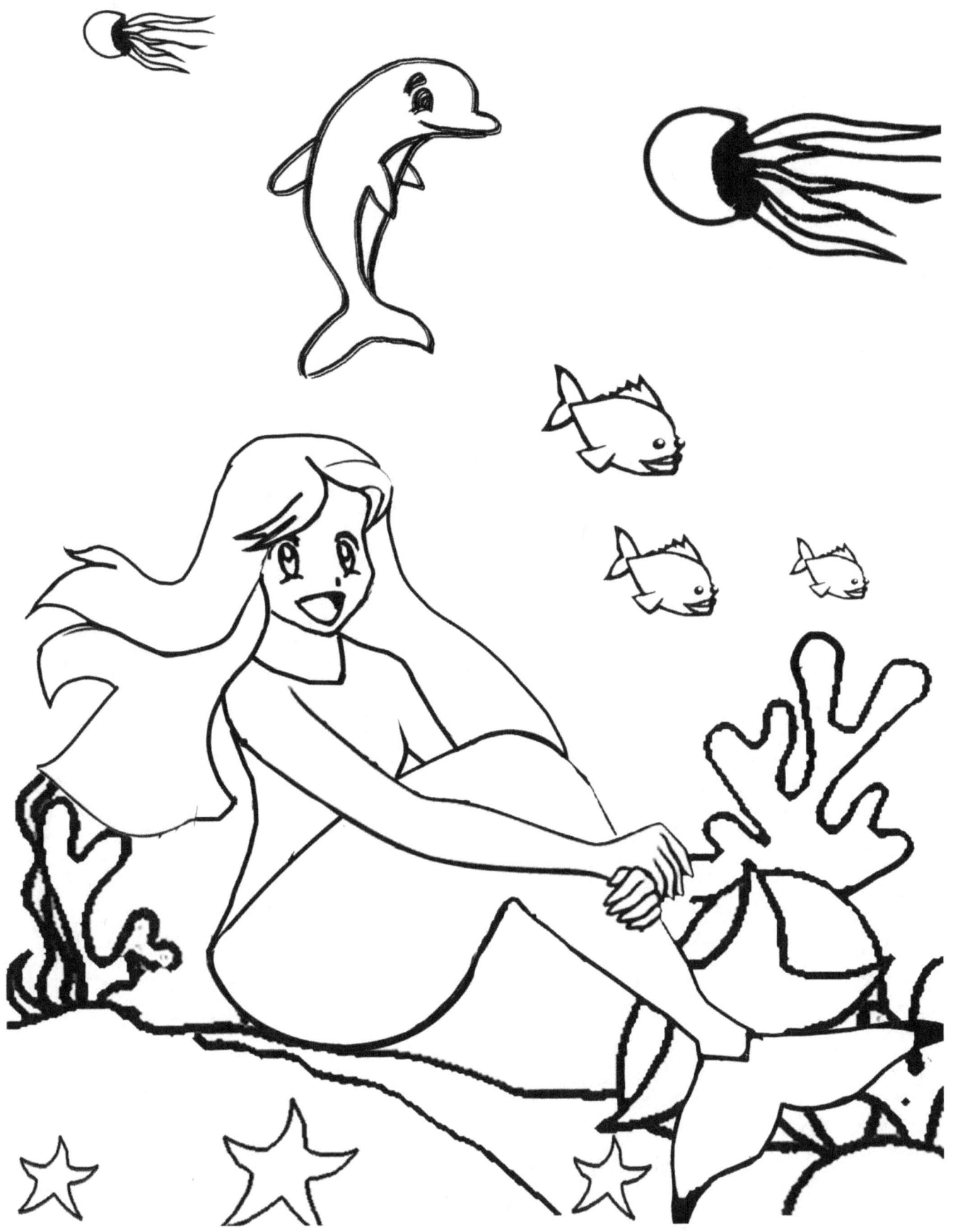

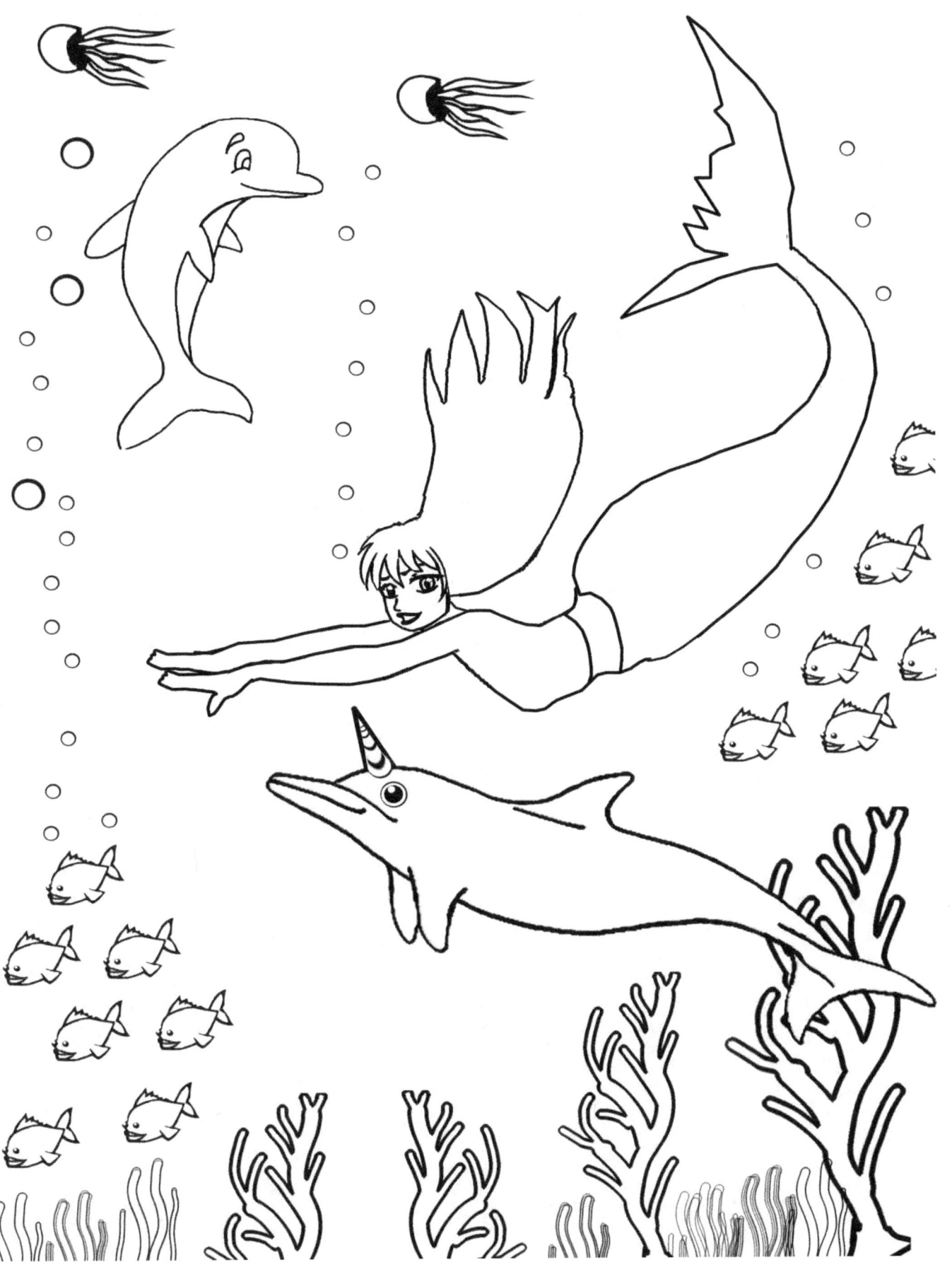

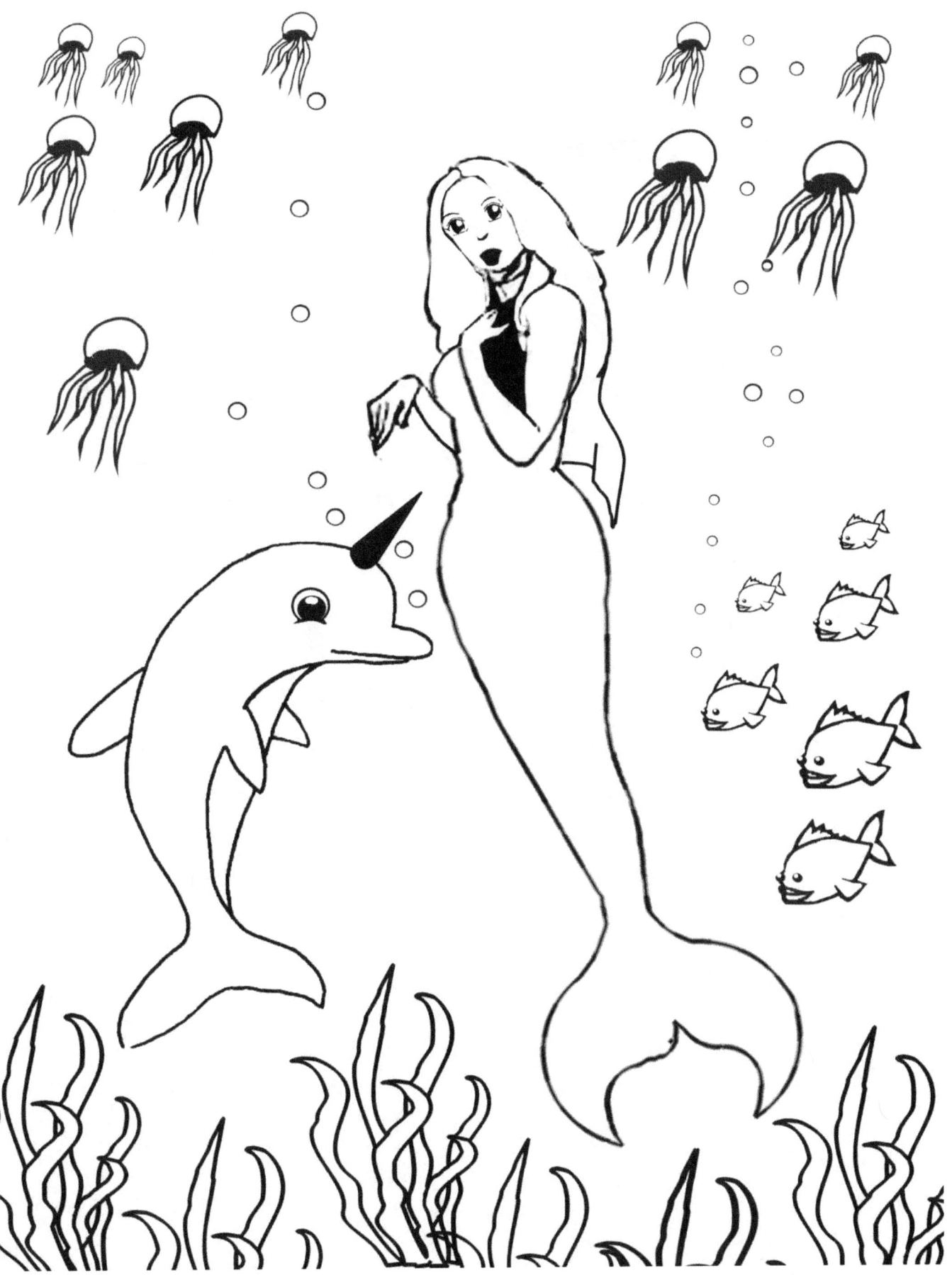

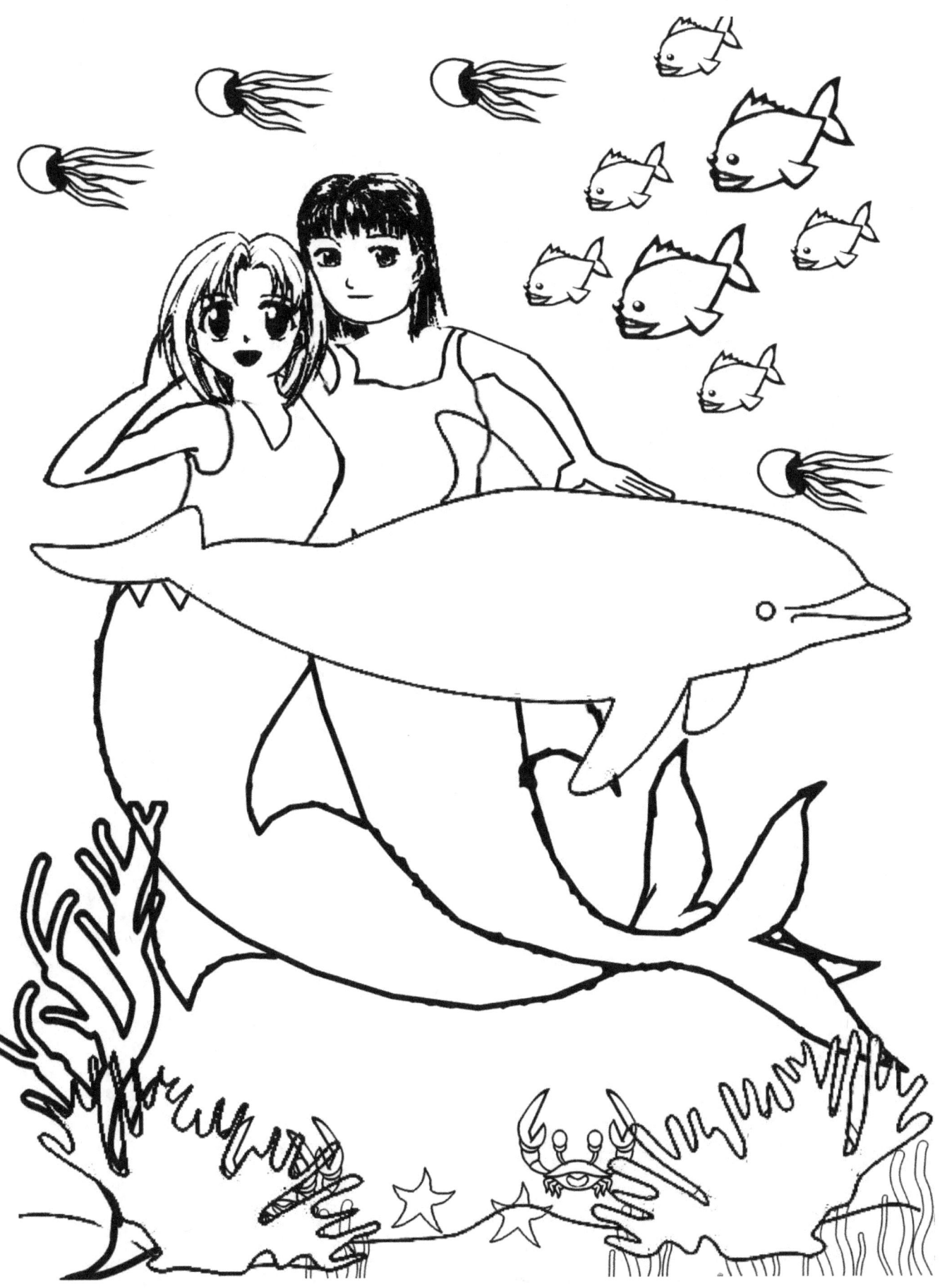

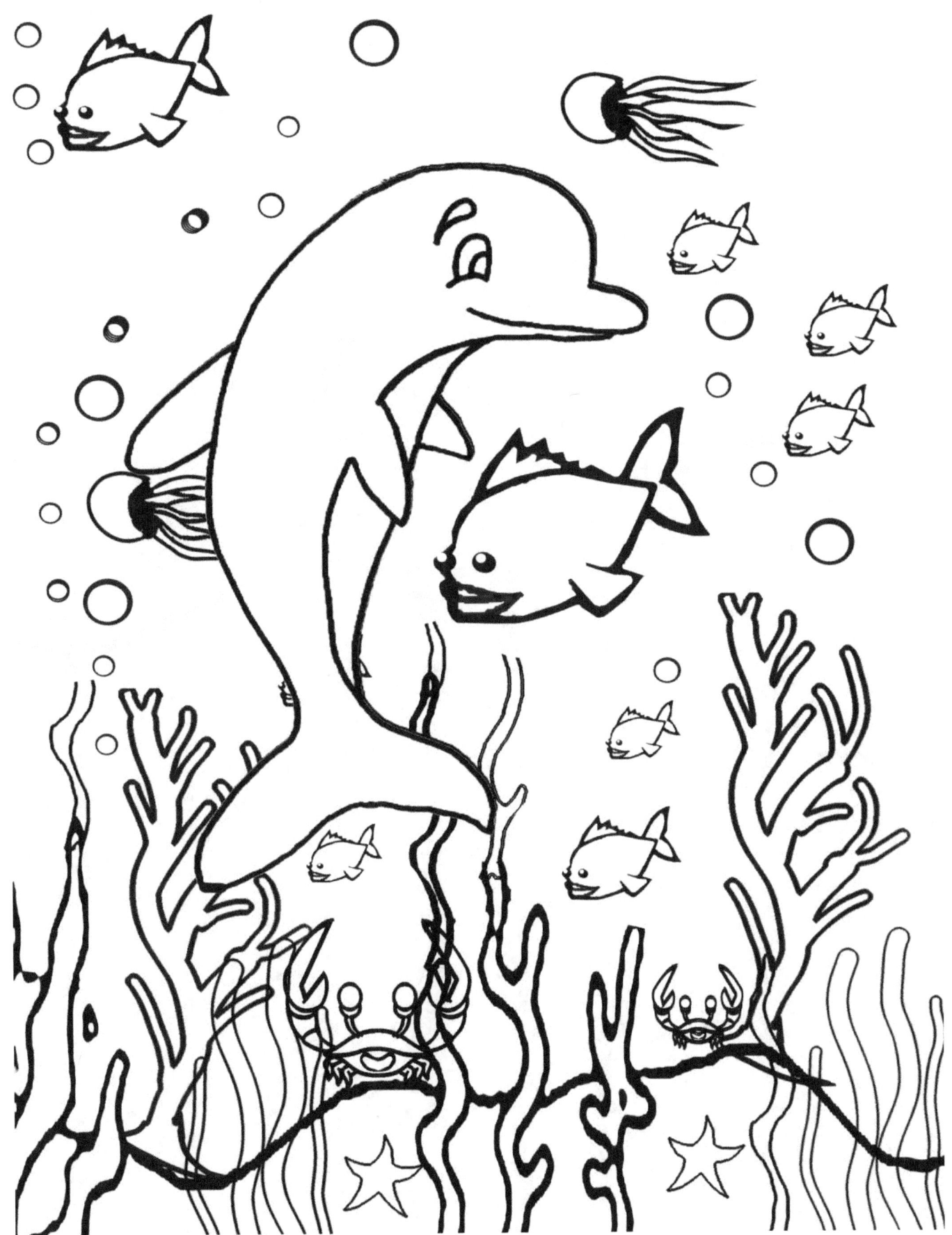

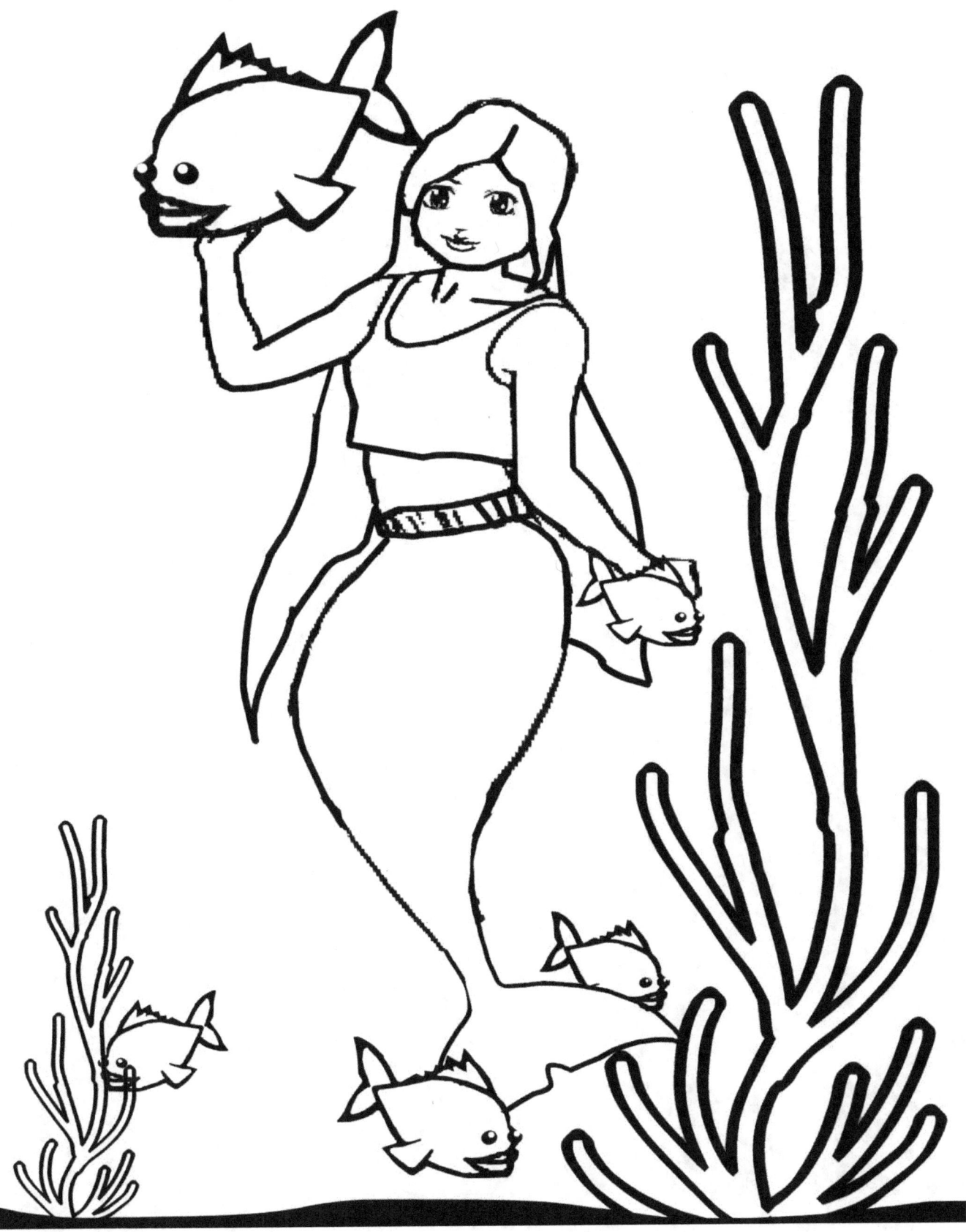

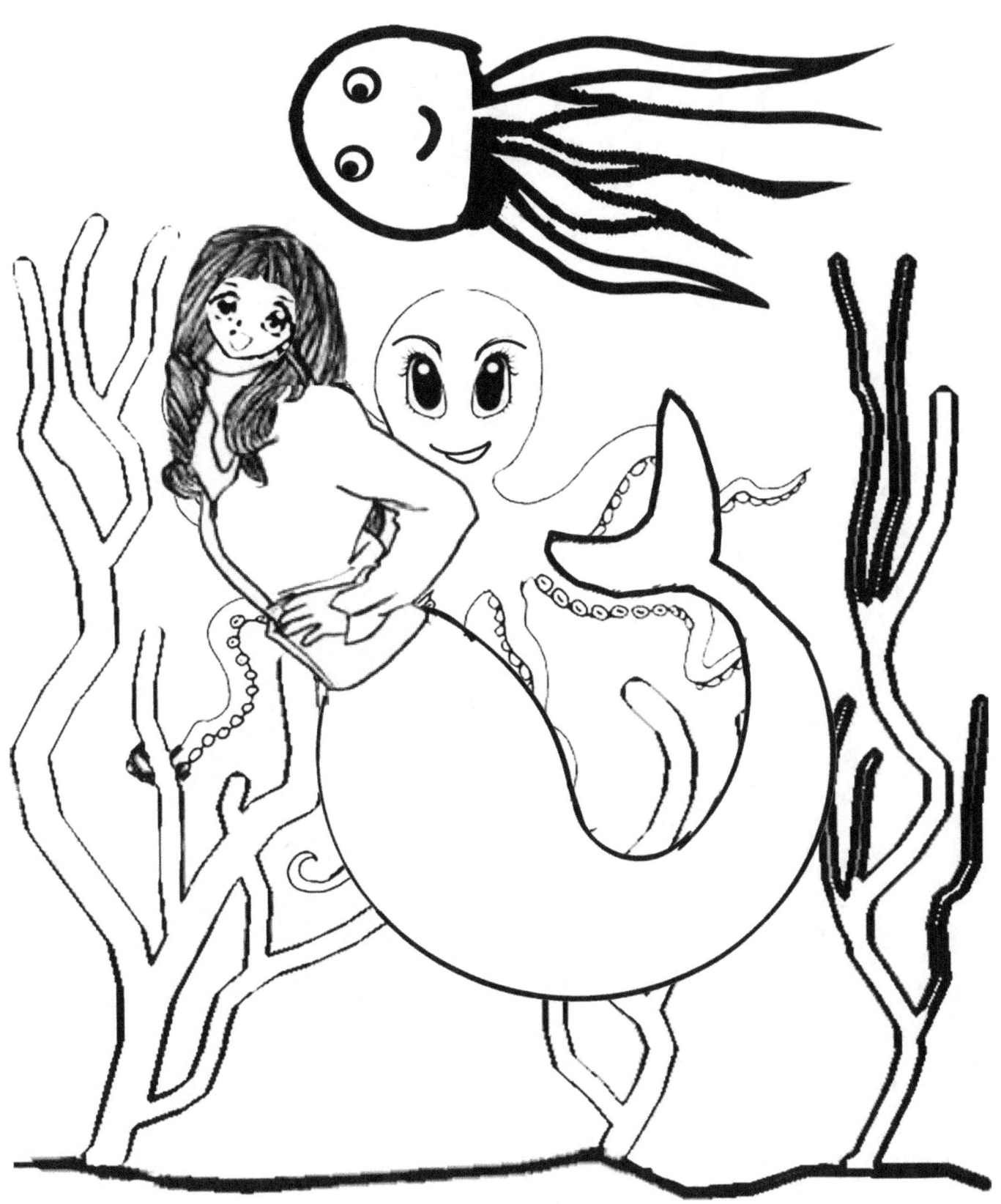

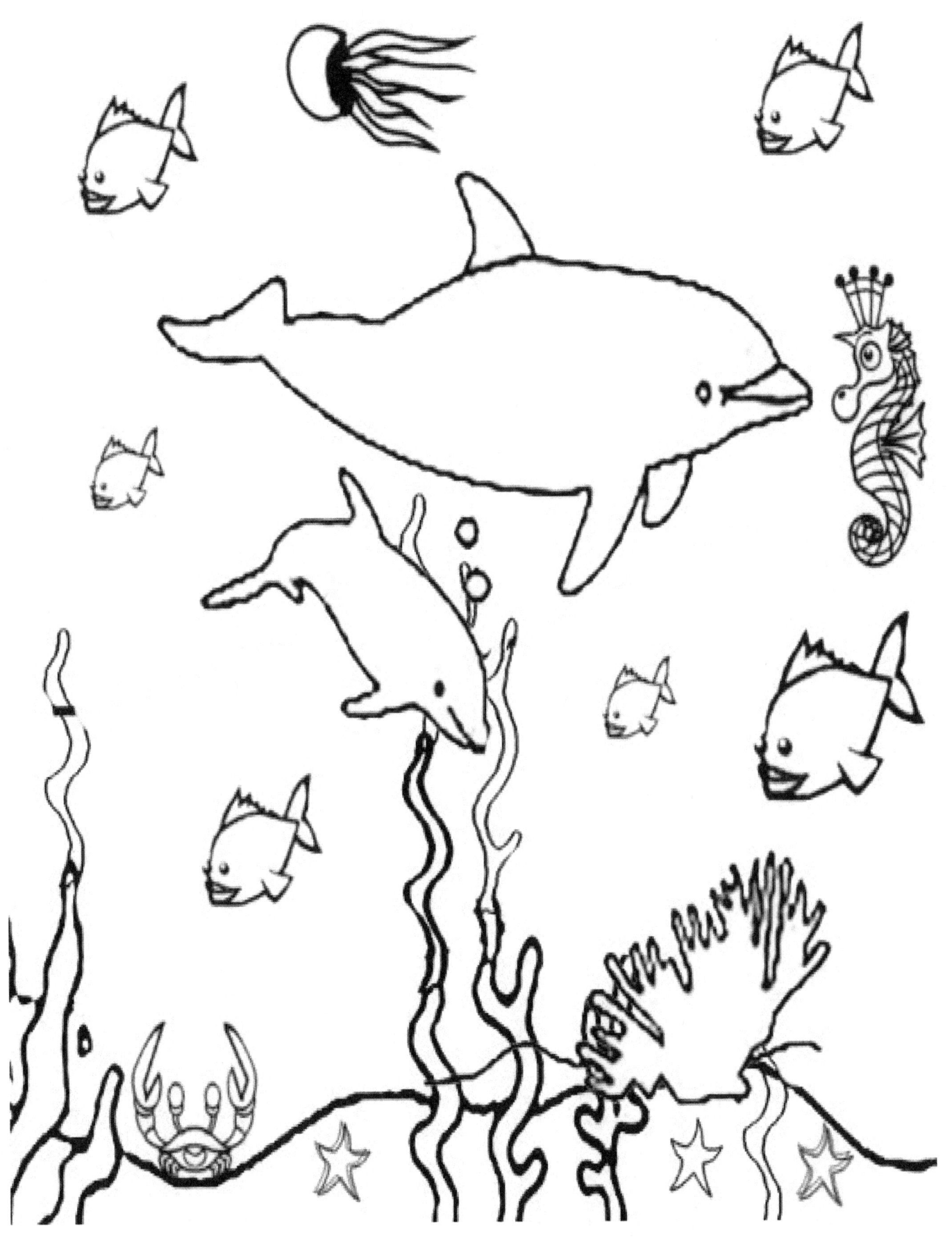

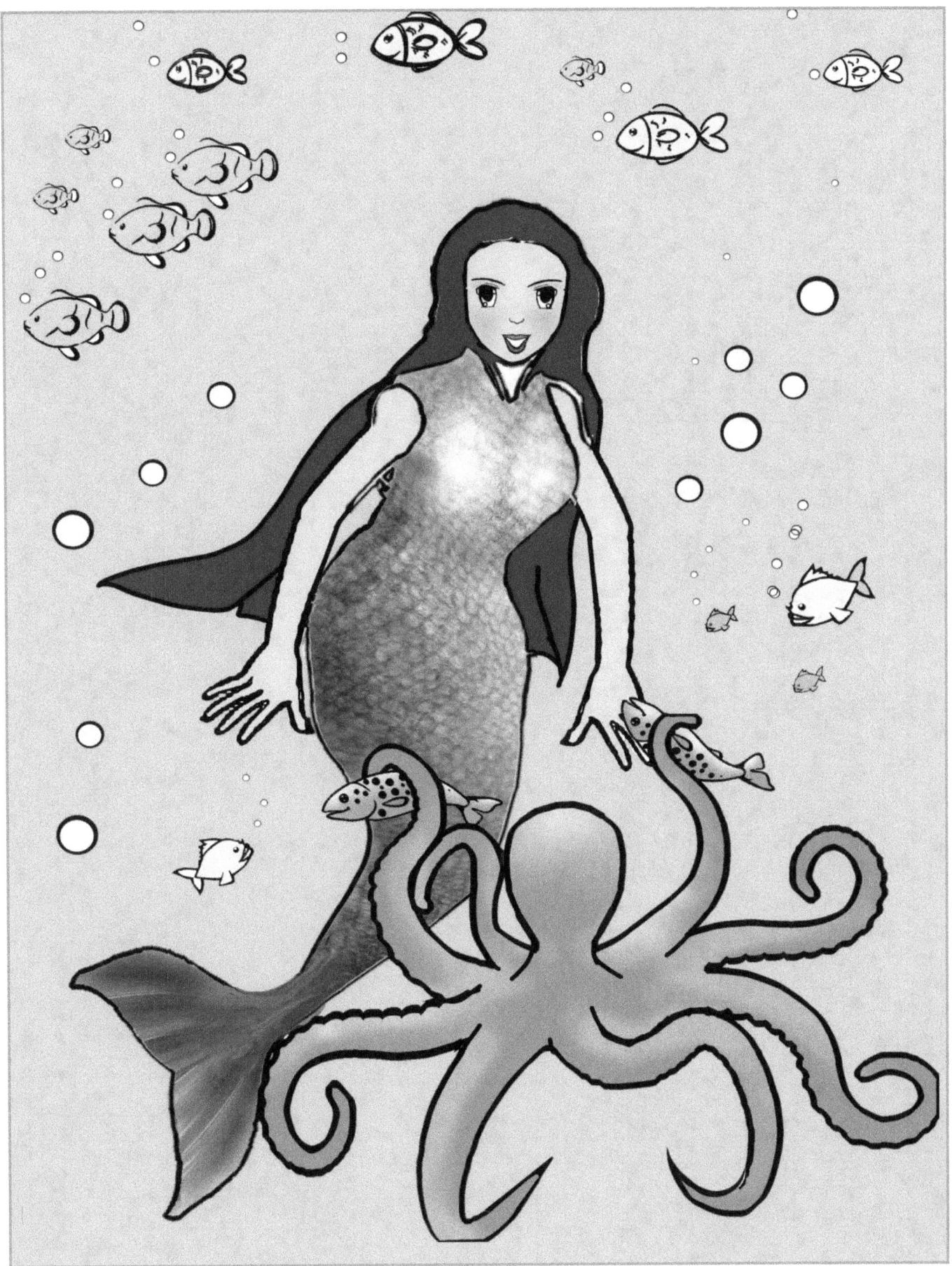

Mermaid and Unicorn dolphin coloring Book

www.ingramcontent.com/pod-product-compliance
Lightning Source LLC
Chambersburg PA
CBHW081102240526
45465CB00026B/3239